D1300833

Yellow Umbrella Books are published by Capstone Press
151 Good Counsel Drive, P.O. Box 669, Mankato, Minnesota 56002
http://www.capstone-press.com

1 2 3 4 5 6 07 06 05 04 03 02

Library of Congress Cataloging-in-Publication Data
Franco, Betsy.
   Many ways to 100/by Betsy Franco
   p. cm. —(Math)
   Includes index.
   Summary: Simple text and photographs show the different ways of counting to 100.
   ISBN 0-7368-1285-7
   1. Counting—Juvenile literature. [1. Counting.] I. Title: Many ways to one hundred.
II. Title. III. Series.
QA113 .F735 2002
513.2′11—dc21
                                           2001008017

Editorial Credits
Susan Evento, Managing Editor/Product Development; Elizabeth Jaffe, Senior Editor; Sidney Wright and Charles Hunt, Designers; Kimberly Danger and Heidi Schoof, Photo Researchers

Photo Credits
Cover: Uniphoto; Table of Contents: (top to bottom) Cathy Gyory, Scott Cambell/International Stock, Cathy Gyory, Fred Reischl/Unicorn Stock Photos; Page 2: Cathy Gyory; Page 3: Cathy Gyory; Page 4: Cathy Gyory; Page 5: Photri; Page 6: International Stock; Page 7: Scott Cambell/International Stock; Page 8: Cathy Gyory; Page 9: Uniphoto; Page 10: Cathy Gyory; Page 11: Cathy Gyory (top and bottom); Page 12: Jack Glisson (top), Cathy Gyory (bottom); Page 13: Cathy Gyory (top, middle, and bottom); Page 14: Fred Reisch/Unicorn Stock; Page 15: Jack Glisson; Page 16: David F. Clobes/Stock Photography (top), Beth Wolf (bottom)

MANY WAYS TO 100

BY BETSY FRANCO

Consulting Editor: Gail Saunders-Smith, Ph.D.
Consultant: Claudine Jellison,
Reading Recovery Teachers
Content Consultant: Johanna Kaufman,
Math Learning/Resource Director of the Dalton School

Yellow Umbrella Books

an imprint of Capstone Press
Mankato, Minnesota

Let's see the different ways
you can count to 100.

You can count 100 little beads.

You can count 100 big beads.

If you want to count to 100,
you can count by 1s.
If you count the marbles
one by one, there would be 100.
"1, 2, 3, 4,...99, 100."

You can count by 2s.
You can count the owls' eyes
in pairs, if you count by 2s.
"2, 4, 6, 8,...98, 100."

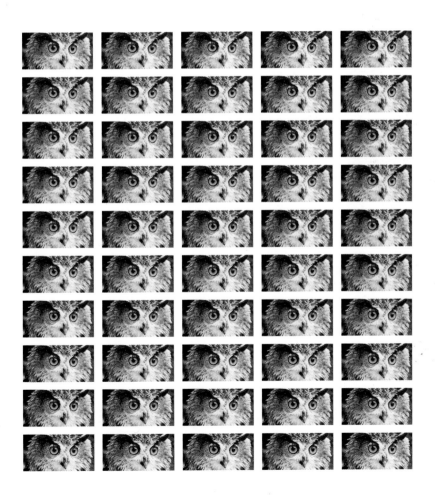

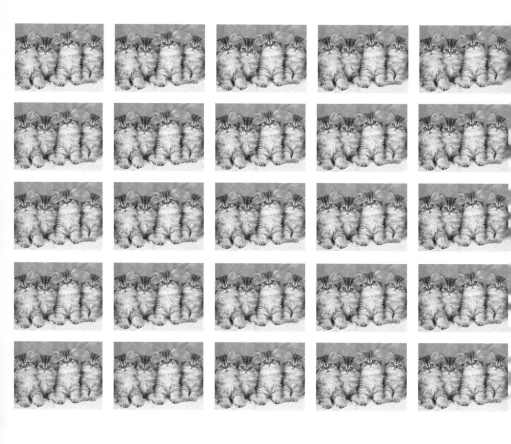

Counting by 4s will get you
to 100 too.
Count the cats grouped by 4s.
"4, 8, 12, 16,...96, 100."

You can get to 100
counting by 5s.
Count the sea star arms by 5s.
"5, 10, 15, 20,...95, 100."

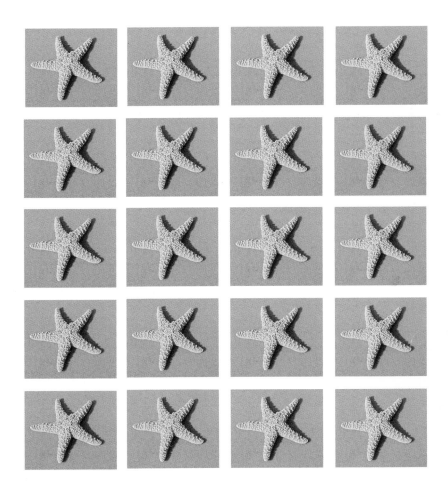

Counting by 10s is a fast way to get to 100.
People have 10 toes.
If you count by 10 for each set of wiggly toes, you are counting by 10s.
"10, 20, 30, 40,...90, 100."

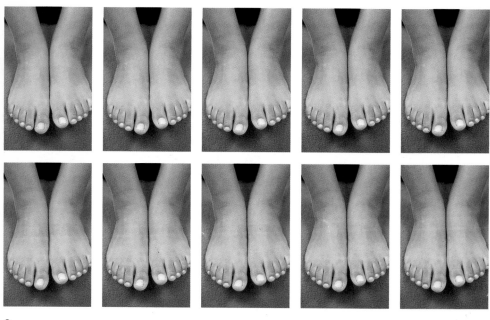

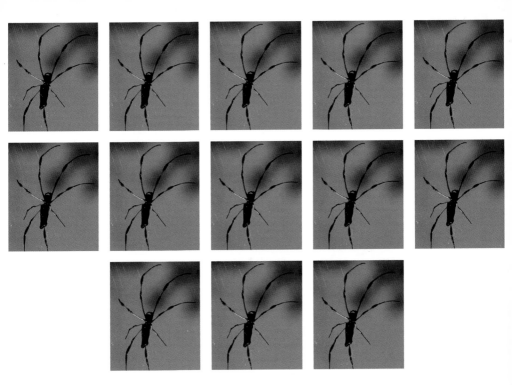

When you count by some
numbers you will never get
exactly to 100.
If you count the spiders' legs
by 8s, you will skip count
from 96 to 104.
"8, 16, 24, 32,...96, 104."

Here's another way to count to 100.
You can count to 100 in rows.
This quilt has 10 rows with
10 squares in each row.
Ten rows of 10 make 100!

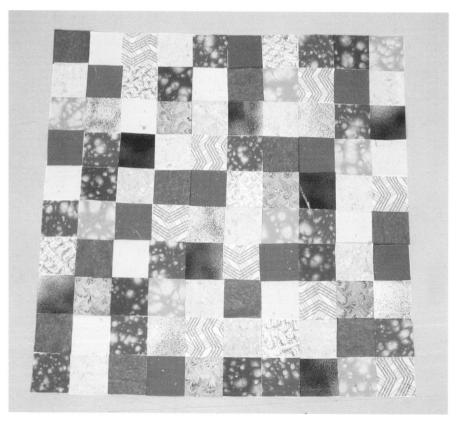

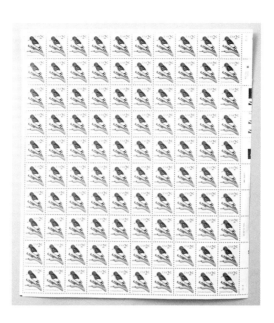

Stamps come in 10 rows
of 10 stamps to make 100.

A roll of stamps can also come
in one long row of 100.

There are many ways
to get to 100¢.
This is 1 dollar.
One dollar is equal to 100¢.

Each penny is worth 1¢.
You can get to 100¢ by counting
100 pennies, one at a time.

Each nickel is worth 5¢.
You can get to 100¢
by counting 20 nickels.

Each dime is worth 10¢.

You can get to 100¢
by counting 10 dimes.

Each quarter is worth 25¢.

You can get to 100¢
by counting 4 quarters.

Counting page by page
is counting by 1s.
Can you find a book
with 100 pages?

If you count book by book,
you can fill a bookcase
with 100 books.
Count them, and you will see!

You can count to the 100th day
of school by counting
each school day.

There are many ways to count
to 100 that are fun!

Words to Know/Index

Word Count: 384
Early-Intervention Level: 15